LITTLE WHISPERS
OF COMFORT
for
Busy Women

BARBOUR
PUBLISHING

Be still, sad heart! And cease repining;
Behind the clouds is the sun still shining.

<small>HENRY WADSWORTH LONGFELLOW</small>

Once you choose hope,
anything's possible.

CHRISTOPHER REEVE

Your worth and purpose in this life do not depend on who you are, on what you have done, or on what has been done to you. . . . Your worth and purpose depend on God and God alone.

Kay Arthur

*C*ount the garden by the flowers,
never by the leaves that fall. Count your life
with smiles and not the tears that roll.

UNKNOWN

$\mathcal{B}$etter to lose count while naming your blessings than to lose your blessings to counting your troubles.

MALTBIE DAVENPORT BABCOCK

$\mathcal{Y}$et, in the maddening maze of things,
And tossed by storm and flood,
To one fixed trust my spirit clings;
I know that God is good!

JOHN GREENLEAF WHITTIER

*C*reativity comes from trust. Trust your instincts.
And never hope more than you work.

RITA MAE BROWN

$\mathcal{N}$o one is more cherished in this world than someone who lightens the burden of another.

UNKNOWN

$\mathcal{T}$o ease another's heartache is to forget one's own.

ABRAHAM LINCOLN

The victory that overcomes the world is our faith, faith in the Good Shepherd. He is our all.

JOHN CAYLOR

$\mathcal{F}$or whatever is born of God overcomes the world;
and this is the victory that has overcome the
world—our faith.

1 JOHN 5:4 NASB

$\mathcal{W}$hen it is dark enough,
you can see the stars.

RALPH WALDO EMERSON

There is in every true woman's heart a spark of heavenly fire, which lies dormant in the broad daylight of prosperity; but which kindles up, and beams and blazes in the dark hour of adversity.

WASHINGTON IRVING

It is a common experience that a problem difficult at night is resolved in the morning after the committee of sleep has worked on it.

JOHN STEINBECK

There is no duty we so underrate as the duty of being happy. By being happy we sow anonymous benefits upon the world.

ROBERT LOUIS STEVENSON

Only those who dare to fail greatly can ever achieve greatly.

Robert F. Kennedy

$\mathcal{D}$ecember is the toughest month of the year. Others are July, January, September, April, November, May, March, June, October, August, and February.

MARK TWAIN

$\mathcal{P}$atience and perseverance have a magical effect
before which difficulties disappear
and obstacles vanish.

JOHN QUINCY ADAMS

*H*istory, despite its wrenching pain, cannot be unlived, but if faced with courage, need not be lived again.

MAYA ANGELOU

If Heaven more generous gifts deny,
I shall not miss them much—
Too grateful for the blessing lent
Of simple tastes and mind content!

OLIVER WENDELL HOLMES

The best remedy for those who are afraid, lonely, or unhappy is to go outside, somewhere where they can be quiet, alone with the heavens, nature, and God. Because only then does one feel that all is as it should be and that God wishes to see people happy, amidst the simple beauty of nature.

ANNE FRANK

$\mathcal{D}$on't be afraid to go out on a limb.
That's where the fruit is.

H. JACKSON BROWNE

I'm not afraid of storms, for I'm learning how to sail my ship.

Louisa May Alcott

If we had no winter, the spring would not be so pleasant; if we did not sometimes taste of adversity, prosperity would not be so welcome.

ANNE BRADSTREET

Love the moment. Flowers grow out of dark moments. Therefore, each moment is vital. It affects the whole. Life is a succession of such moments; and to live each, is to succeed.

CORITA KENT

"When you pass through the waters, I will be with you; and when you pass through the rivers, they will not sweep over you. When you walk through the fire, you will not be burned; the flames will not set you ablaze. For I am the LORD, your God."

ISAIAH 43:2–3 NIV

*N*ever apologize for showing feeling. When you do so, you apologize for the truth.

Benjamin Disraeli

And as we let our own light shine,
we unconsciously give other people
permission to do the same.

MARIANNE WILLIAMSON

$\mathcal{T}$he best and most beautiful things in the world
cannot be seen, nor touched. . .
but are felt in the heart.

HELEN KELLER

I am thankful for a lawn that needs mowing,
windows that need cleaning, and gutters that need
fixing because it means I have a home. . . .
I am thankful for the piles of laundry and ironing
because it means my loved ones are nearby.

NANCIE J. CARMODY

$\mathcal{T}$here is only one happiness in life,
to love and be loved.

GEORGE SAND

The road that is built in hope is more pleasant
to the traveler than the road built in despair,
even though they both lead
to the same destination.

MARION ZIMMER BRADLEY

It is not the mountain we conquer but ourselves.

SIR EDMUND HILLARY

$\mathcal{W}$hen you get into a tight place and everything goes against you, till it seems as though you could not hold on a minute longer, never give up then, for that is just the place and time that the tide will turn.

HARRIET BEECHER STOWE

I ask not for a lighter burden,
but for broader shoulders.

JEWISH PROVERB

It is foolish to tear one's hair in grief, as though sorrow would be made less by baldness.

CICERO

*E*very problem has in it the seeds of its own solution. If you don't have any problems, you don't get any seeds.

NORMAN VINCENT PEALE

*I*f you can bear to hear the truth you've spoken
Twisted by knaves to make a trap for fools,
Or watch the things you gave your life to broken,
And stoop and build 'em up with wornout tools. . .
Yours is the Earth and everything that's in it.

Rudyard Kipling

$\mathcal{T}$here is nothing stronger in the
world than gentleness.

HAN SUYIN

$Giving$ up doesn't always mean you are weak;
sometimes it means that you are
strong enough to let go.

UNKNOWN

That is why, for Christ's sake, I delight in
weaknesses, in insults, in hardships,
in persecutions, in difficulties.
For when I am weak, then I am strong.

2 Corinthians 12:10 NIV

Happiness is as a butterfly which, when pursued, is always beyond your grasp, but which if you will sit down quietly, may alight upon you.

NATHANIEL HAWTHORNE

*S*ometimes your joy is the source of your smile, but sometimes your smile can be the source of your joy.

THICH NHAT HANH

Perhaps everything terrible is in its deepest being
something helpless that wants help from us.

RAINER MARIA RILKE

The seed of joy grows best in a field of peace.

ROBERT J. WICKS

*T*hose who bring sunshine into the lives of others
cannot keep it from themselves.

J. M. BARRIE

Success is not the key to happiness. Happiness is the key to success. If you love what you are doing, you will be successful.

ALBERT SCHWEITZER

*O*ne act of beneficence, one act of real usefulness,
is worth all the abstract sentiment in the world.

Ann Radcliffe

A life spent making mistakes is not only more honorable, but more useful than a life spent in doing nothing.

GEORGE BERNARD SHAW

The difficulties of life are intended to make us better, not bitter.

UNKNOWN

By perseverance the snail reached the ark.

CHARLES H. SPURGEON

$\mathcal{B}$eautiful shoulders are those that bear
Ceaseless burdens of homely care
With patient grace and daily prayer.

ELLEN P. ALLERTON

The difference between perseverance and obstinacy is that one comes from a strong will, and the other from a strong won't.

HENRY WARD BEECHER

When you come to the end of your rope,
tie a knot and hang on.

FRANKLIN D. ROOSEVELT

Consider the postage stamp: its usefulness consists in the ability to stick to one thing till it gets there.

JOSH BILLINGS

Therefore, since we have so great a cloud of witnesses surrounding us, let us also lay aside every encumbrance and the sin which so easily entangles us, and let us run with endurance the race that is set before us.

HEBREWS 12:1 NASB

Giving frees us from the familiar territory of our own needs by opening our mind to the unexplained worlds occupied by the needs of others.

Barbara Bush

You make a living by what you get.
You make a life by what you give.

WINSTON CHURCHILL

At times our own light goes out and is rekindled by a spark from another person. Each of us has cause to think with deep gratitude of those who have lighted the flame within us.

ALBERT SCHWEITZER

For life is the mirror of king and slave—
'Tis just what we are and do;
Then give to the world the best you have,
And the best will come back to you.

MADELINE BRIDGES

$\mathcal{H}$appiness cannot be traveled to, owned, earned, worn, or consumed. Happiness is the spiritual experience of living every minute with love, grace, and gratitude.

DENIS WAITLEY

How wonderful it is that nobody need wait a single moment before starting to improve the world.

ANNE FRANK

$\mathcal{D}$o good by stealth, and blush to find it fame.

ALEXANDER POPE

Do all the good you can, by all the means you can,
in all the ways you can, in all the places you can,
at all the times you can, to all the people you can,
as long as ever you can.

JOHN WESLEY

Those who try to do something and fail are infinitely better than those who try nothing and succeed.

LLOYD JONES

$Getting$ what you go after is success;
but liking it while you are getting it is happiness.

BERTHA DAMON

*B*alance, peace, and joy are the fruit of a successful life. It starts with recognizing your talents and finding ways to serve others by using them.

THOMAS KINKADE

$\mathcal{T}$he habit of giving only enhances the desire to give.

WALT WHITMAN

I asked for all things, that I might enjoy life;
I was given life that I might enjoy all things. . .
I got nothing that I asked for—but everything
I had hoped for.

UNKNOWN

*L*ove conquers more enemies than soldiers can. Love opens more doors than battering rams can burst open. Love opens doors of opportunity where money, influence, and power fail. . . . "God is love."

<small>JOHN CAYLOR</small>

We know how much God loves us, and we have put our trust in his love. God is love, and all who live in love live in God, and God lives in them. Such love has no fear, because perfect love expels all fear.

1 John 4:16, 18 nlt

No heaven can come to us unless our hearts find rest in it today. Take heaven! No peace lies in the future which is not hidden in this present little instant. Take peace!

Fra Giovanni Giocondo

$\mathcal{L}$ord, make me an instrument of your peace;
where there is hatred, let me sow love;
where there is injury, pardon;
where there is doubt, faith;
where there is despair, hope;
where there is darkness, light;
and where there is sadness, joy.

ST. FRANCIS OF ASSISI

In three words I can sum up everything I've learned about life: it goes on.

ROBERT FROST

$\mathcal{W}$hen some great sorrow, like a mighty river,
Flows through your life with
peace-destroying power. . .
Say to your heart each trying hour:
"This, too, shall pass away."

LANTA WILSON SMITH

It is hard to fail, but it is worse
never to have tried to succeed.

THEODORE ROOSEVELT

The value of life lies not in the length of days,
but in the use we make of them.

MICHEL DE MONTAIGNE

I have learned over the years that when one's mind is made up, this diminishes fear; knowing what must be done does away with fear.

ROSA PARKS

$\mathcal{A}$daptable as human beings are and have to be,
I sometimes sympathize with the chameleon who
had a nervous breakdown on a patchwork quilt.

JOHN STEPHEN STRANGE

The world is divided into people who do things and people who get the credit. Try, if you can, to belong to the first class. There's far less competition.

DWIGHT MORROW

If you have made mistakes, there is always another chance for you. You may have a fresh start any moment you choose, for this thing we call "failure" is not the falling down, but the staying down.

MARY PICKFORD

*A*im above morality. Be not simply good;
be good for something.

Henry David Thoreau

There cannot be a crisis next week.
My schedule is already full.

HENRY KISSINGER

Kindness is the language which the deaf can hear and the blind can see.

MARK TWAIN

$Gratefulness$ is the key to a happy life that we hold in our hands, because if we are not grateful, then no matter how much we have we will not be happy—because we will always want to have something else or something more.

BROTHER DAVID STEINDL-RAST

Godliness actually is a means of great gain when accompanied by contentment. For we have brought nothing into the world, so we cannot take anything out of it either. If we have food and covering, with these we shall be content.

1 TIMOTHY 6:6–8 NASB

$\mathcal{T}$he supreme happiness in life is the conviction that we are loved.

Victor Hugo

*G*ratitude is the fairest blossom which springs from the soul.

HENRY WARD BEECHER

*I*t matters not how deep entrenched the wrong,
How hard the battle goes, the day how long;
Faint not—fight on! Tomorrow comes the song.

Maltbie Davenport Babcock

Mountaintops inspire leaders,
but valleys mature them.

WINSTON CHURCHILL

$\mathcal{A}$ge is nothing but experience, and some of us are more experienced than others.

ANDY ROONEY

$\mathcal{G}$ood judgment is usually the result of experience.
And experience is frequently the result
of bad judgment.

UNKNOWN

Maturity of mind is the capacity
to endure uncertainty.

JOHN FINLEY

The harder the conflict, the more glorious the triumph.

Thomas Paine

$\mathcal{W}$e could never learn to be brave and patient if there were only joy in the world.

HELEN KELLER

A thousand unseen hands
Reach down to help you to their
peace-crowned heights,
And all the forces of the firmament
Shall fortify your strength.

ELLA WHEELER WILCOX

Occasionally in life there are moments. . .
which cannot be completely explained by words.
Their meaning can only be articulated by the
inaudible language of the heart.

MARTIN LUTHER KING JR.

*O*ne sad thing about this world is that the acts that take the most out of you are usually the ones that other people will never know about.

ANNE TYLER

$\mathcal{T}$o enjoy yourself is the easy method to give
enjoyment to others.

L. E. LANDON

$\mathcal{L}$ove is a great thing, a great good in every way;
it alone lightens what is heavy and leads smoothly
over all roughness.

THOMAS À KEMPIS

$\mathcal{L}$ove is patient, love is kind and is not jealous; love. . .bears all things, believes all things, hopes all things, endures all things. Love never fails.

1 CORINTHIANS 13:4,7−8 NASB

*L*et nothing disturb thee;
Let nothing dismay thee;
All things pass;
God never changes.

St. Teresa of Avila

Jesus did not say, "You will never have a rough passage, you will never be over-strained, you will never feel uncomfortable," but He did say, "You will never be overcome."

JULIAN OF NORWICH

$\mathcal{T}$o speak gratitude is courteous and pleasant, to enact gratitude is generous and noble, but to live gratitude is to touch heaven.

JOHANNES A. GAERTNER

$\mathcal{W}$e may encounter defeats, but we
must not be defeated.

MAYA ANGELOU

$Dreams$ are. . .illustrations from the book your soul is writing about you.

MARSHA NORMAN

$\mathcal{L}$et us gather up the sunbeams
Lying all around our path;
Let us keep the wheat and roses,
Casting out the thorns and chaff.

MAY RILEY SMITH

The thought that we are enduring the unendurable is one of the things that keep us going.

Molly Haskell

Problems are only opportunities in work clothes.

HENRY J. KAISER

$\mathcal{A}$ single candle can light a thousand more without diminishing itself.

HILLEL THE ELDER

$\mathcal{W}$hile there's life, there's hope.

THEOCRITUS

Fight on, though ye bleed in the trial,
Resist with all strength that ye may. . . .
Walk with faith, and be sure you'll get through it;
For "Where there's a will there's a way."

ELIZA COOK

*I*n the past we have had a light which flickered,
in the present we have a light which flames,
and in the future there will be a light which shines
over all the land and sea.

WINSTON CHURCHILL

$\mathcal{P}$rosperity is not without many fears and disasters; and adversity is not without comforts and hopes.

FRANCIS BACON

$\mathcal{W}$e have always held to the hope, the belief, the conviction, that there is a better life, a better world, beyond the horizon.

FRANKLIN D. ROOSEVELT

$\mathcal{F}$or I am convinced that neither death, nor life, nor angels, nor principalities, nor things present, nor things to come, nor powers, nor height, nor depth, nor any other created thing, will be able to separate us from the love of God, which is in Christ Jesus our Lord.

ROMANS 8:38–39 NASB

$\mathcal{L}$ove is devoted and thankful to God, always
trusting and hoping in Him, even when it doesn't
taste His sweetness, for without pain
no one can live in love.

THOMAS À KEMPIS

$\mathcal{L}$earning to live with what you're born with is the process, the involvement, the making of a life.

Diane Wakoski

$\mathcal{N}$obody made a greater mistake than he who did nothing because he could do only a little.

EDMUND BURKE

Each kindly act is an acorn dropped
In God's productive soil;
You may not know, but the tree shall grow
With shelter for those who toil.

ELLA WHEELER WILCOX

*I*f you're frightened, don't sit still, keep on doing something. The act of doing will give you back your courage.

GRACE OGOT

*G*ratitude unlocks the fullness of life.
It turns what we have into enough, and more.

MELODIE BEATTIE

$\mathcal{A}$bundance is, in large part, an attitude.

SUE PATTON THOELE

Every great dream begins with a dreamer. Always remember, you have within you the strength, the patience, and the passion to reach for the stars to change the world.

HARRIET TUBMAN

I don't waste time thinking,
"Am I doing it right?" I ask,
"Am I doing it?"

GEORGETTE MOSBACHER

$\mathcal{W}$e cannot live for ourselves alone. Our lives are connected by a thousand invisible threads, and along these sympathetic fibers, our actions run as causes and return to us as results.

HERMAN MELVILLE

$\mathcal{B}$eautiful eyes are those that show,
Like crystal panes where hearthfires glow,
Beautiful thoughts that burn below.

ELLEN P. ALLERTON

The gloom of the world is but a shadow. Behind it, yet within our reach, is joy. There is radiance and glory in the darkness, could we but see; and to see, we have only to look.

FRA GIOVANNI GIOCONDO

Sow an act and you reap a habit; sow a habit and you reap a character; sow a character and you reap a destiny.

FRANCES E. WILLARD

*G*od has not called me to be successful;
he has called me to be faithful.

MOTHER TERESA

For I am confident of this very thing, that He who began a good work in you will perfect it until the day of Christ Jesus.

PHILIPPIANS 1:6 NASB

We must accept finite disappointment,
but we must never lose infinite hope.

MARTIN LUTHER KING JR.

$\mathcal{D}$on't waste life in doubts and fears; spend yourself on the work before you, well assured that the right performance of this hour's duties will be the best preparation for the hours and ages that will follow it.

RALPH WALDO EMERSON

Only when we are no longer afraid do
we begin to live.

DOROTHY THOMPSON

$\mathcal{T}$o fear is one thing. To let fear grab you by the tail and swing you around is another.

KATHERINE PATERSON

*Flops are a part of life's menu,
and I've never been a girl
to miss out on any of the courses.*

ROSALIND RUSSELL

There is no chance, no destiny, no fate,
Can circumvent or hinder or control
The firm resolve of a determined soul.

ELLA WHEELER WILCOX

$\mathcal{N}$ot failure, but low aim, is crime.

JAMES RUSSELL LOWELL

$\mathcal{I}$f you lose hope, somehow you lose the vitality that keeps life moving, you lose that courage to be, that quality that helps you go on in spite of it all. And so today I still have a dream.

MARTIN LUTHER KING JR.

$\mathcal{P}$roblems are not stop signs, they are guidelines.

Robert Schuller

I have no fear, though strait the gate,
He cleared from punishment the scroll.
Christ is the Master of my fate,
Christ is the Captain of my soul.

WILLIAM ERNEST HENLEY

The greater the difficulty, the more glory in surmounting it. Skillful pilots gain their reputation from storms and tempests.

EPICURUS

$\mathcal{W}$ithout leaps of imagination, or dreaming,
we lose the excitement of possibilities. Dreaming,
after all, is a form of planning.

GLORIA STEINEM

The greatest glory in living lies not in never falling, but in rising every time we fall.

NELSON MANDELA

$\mathcal{F}$all seven times, stand up eight.

JAPANESE PROVERB

Yet those who wait for the LORD will gain new strength; they will mount up with wings like eagles, they will run and not get tired, they will walk and not become weary.

ISAIAH 40:31 NASB

$\mathcal{A}$lthough the world is full of suffering, it is full also of the overcoming of it.

HELEN KELLER

$\mathcal{W}$hen one's own problems are unsolvable, and all best efforts frustrated, it is lifesaving to listen to other people's problems.

Suzanne Massie

$\mathcal{P}$rayer is a long rope with a strong hold.

HARRIET BEECHER STOWE

$\mathcal{W}$e are building in sorrow or joy
A temple the world may not see,
Which time cannot mar nor destroy;
We build for eternity.

N. B. Sargent

$\mathcal{P}$atience is bitter, but its fruit is sweet.

JEAN JACQUES ROUSSEAU

$\mathcal{T}$hose who've never rebelled against God,
or at some point in their lives
shaken their fists in the face of heaven,
have never encountered God at all.

CATHERINE MARSHALL

$\mathcal{I}$t is not given to everyone to shine in adversity.

JANE AIKEN HODGE

In the middle of every difficulty lies opportunity.

ALBERT EINSTEIN

Pray inwardly, even if you do not enjoy it. It does good, though you feel nothing. Yes, even though you think you are doing nothing.

JULIAN OF NORWICH

When we were children,
we used to think that when we were grown-up
we would no longer be vulnerable.
But to grow up is to accept vulnerability.

MADELEINE L'ENGLE

$\mathcal{N}$o soul is desolate as long as there is a human being for whom it can feel trust and reverence.

GEORGE ELIOT

It is of immense importance to learn
to laugh at ourselves.

KATHERINE MANSFIELD

$\mathcal{T}$hink still of lovely things that are not true.
Let wish and magic work at will in you.
Be sometimes blind to sorrow. Make believe!

LOUISE DRISCOLL

$\mathcal{D}$aring ideas are like chessmen moved forward;
they may be beaten, but they may
start a winning game.

JOHANN WOLFGANG VON GOETHE

"May the LORD reward your work, and your wages be full from the LORD, the God of Israel, under whose wings you have come to seek refuge."

RUTH 2:12 NASB

Only as high as I reach can I grow, only as far as I seek can I go, only as deep as I look can I see, only as much as I dream can I be.

KAREN RAVN

$\mathcal{W}$hen I hear music, I fear no danger. I am invulnerable. I see no foe. I am related to the earliest times, and to the latest.

HENRY DAVID THOREAU

Acknowledge nature—take a walk or look out the window. Write something every day. Have a sensory experience of touching a flower, tree bark, or a leaf. Put aside some pampering time each day to do something special for yourself.
Smile at everyone you meet.

LADY OF LIGHT

God is our clothing that wraps, clasps, and encloses
us so as to never leave us.

JULIAN OF NORWICH

$\mathcal{A}$lways do right. This will gratify some people, and astonish the rest.

MARK TWAIN

$\mathcal{L}$ife is so generous a giver; but we, judging its gifts by their covering, cast them away as ugly or heavy or hard. Remove the covering, and you will find beneath it a living splendor, woven of love, by wisdom, with power.

FRA GIOVANNI GIOCONDO

I long to accomplish a great and noble task, but it is my chief duty to accomplish humble tasks as though they were great and noble. The world is moved along, not only by the mighty shoves of its heroes, but also by the aggregate of the tiny pushes of each honest worker.

HELEN KELLER

Incredible things can happen as long as you keep your mind open and your intentions pure. Change can be a second chance at life.

Rayna Stark

Act, and God will act.

JOAN OF ARC

I begin to think that a calm is not desirable in any situation in life. . . . [We were] made for action and for bustle too, I believe.

ABIGAIL ADAMS

In a society that judges self-worth on productivity, it's no wonder we fall prey to the misconception that the more we do, the more we're worth.

ELLEN SUE STERN

$\mathcal{W}$ouldn't this old world be better
If the folks we meet would say—
"I know something good about you!"
And treat us just that way?

LOUIS C. SHIMON

$\mathcal{M}$ost of us, swimming against the tides of trouble the world knows nothing about, need only a bit of praise or encouragement—and we will make the goal.

JEROME FLEISHMAN

My most spectacular answers to prayer have come when I was so helpless, so out of control as to be able to do nothing at all for myself.

CATHERINE MARSHALL

And the Holy Spirit helps us in our weakness.
For example, we don't know what God wants us to
pray for. But the Holy Spirit prays for us
with groanings that cannot be
expressed in words.

ROMANS 8:26 NLT

Endurance is not just the ability to bear a hard thing, but to turn it into glory.

WILLIAM BARCLAY

God is not in the vastness of greatness. He is hid in the vastness of smallness. He is not in the general. He is in the particular.

Pearl S. Buck

$\mathcal{H}$uman life nearly resembles iron. When you use it, it wears out. When you don't, rust consumes it.

Cato the Elder

If I rest, I rust.

MARTIN LUTHER

$\mathcal{N}$o one, Eleanor Roosevelt said, can make you feel inferior without your consent. Never give it.

MARIAN WRIGHT EDELMAN

I believe that God is in me as the sun is in the color and fragrance of a flower—the Light in my darkness, the Voice in my silence.

HELEN KELLER

It doesn't matter how small the beginning may seem to be; what is once done well is done forever.

HENRY DAVID THOREAU

Start by doing what's necessary; then do what's
possible; and suddenly you are
doing the impossible.

ST. FRANCIS OF ASSISI

Just start to sing as you tackle the thing
That "cannot be done" and you'll do it.

EDGAR A. GUEST

Twenty years from now you will be more disappointed by the things that you didn't do than by the ones you did do. So throw off the bowlines. Sail away from the safe harbor. Catch the trade winds in your sails. Explore. Dream. Discover.

MARK TWAIN